Juliology

Counterpath Press
Denver, Colorado
2008

Juliology

Nicolas Pesquès

Translated from the French by Cole Swensen

Counterpath Press
Denver, Colorado
www.counterpathpress.org

Printed in the United States of America

Library of Congress Cataloging-in-Publication Data

Pesquès, Nicolas.
  [Juliologie. English]
  Juliology / Nicolas Pesquès ; translated by Cole Swensen.
    p.   cm.
  ISBN 978-1-933996-08-0 (pbk. : alk. paper)
  I. Swensen, Cole, 1955– II. Title.
PQ2676.E7829J813 2008
841'.914—dc22
                                    2008030068

Distributed by Small Press Distribution (www.spdbooks.org)

Juliology

I

Writing: it's the same thing except for time
the same spontaneous force minus the shock
plus that of having the words all together for once.

there is no reprieve in the field, nor in prose
no yellow   except the exact grass
nor transport

while the hill thins out
color hardens, cruel, adjectival,

the same iceberg under the skirts of the sentence.

. . .

in the stand of broom, we watch
the headlong flight of the very sharp and the very flock

this mix of perfect life and active silence
I invent its memory with the same stunned air
the same superb yellow

on this earth full of the tangible and the vertiginous
it's the word that wants it all
that animist
the hook of orgasm, the grip

to note the ways in which the yellow broom is similar
in this marble moment
in this love engraved

with its definitions carved into the bark
austere, precise
and so warmly alive

there where it rustles, on the bridged slope
retracted by the acidic

. . .

"don't tell me tales"
"tell me the truth"
as if the two diverged
and we weren't always trying to come up with a single version

a version made impossible by language

by the autonomy of grammar

yellow even though *yellow*

it's always written as

from a long right-angled petition
the yellow of the room gleaming with English broom

and at the end, a sentence that
as it cools down
continues streaming,

raises the hill

the steel limestone
the wealth of twist and flex

in headstrong yellow

and so an instant can only really get intense
through forceful construction
forcefully knotted

and its emotion is only rooted
in the certainty of accident

though also in escaping it.

. . .

traces of resin in tenderness,
crossing the forest's brambling plush

tenderness reduced to its own acceleration

linen's song
oriole's wall

this is a shore

an onrushing crowd, dispersed
a brilliance that bows down to brilliance

while in fact, I can go back no farther than constriction, poison
and bliss

. . .

our ancestors are simply there, in the sentence
forgotten
they're there in the color
rebelling in the very language of their propagation

which is played out in pain

and there is also the young, fine-ankled yellow

sever and resurge

the more I look at the landscape
the more I hear the words' dissent

as if a gorgeous separation
resounded

as if we could shape letters from light

and if lots of these leaps are due solely to my femininity,
to the yellow I want to enclose between my knees

the hill's verso
which buries me up to real nature
to my sister physis

the atomic and the anatomic

. . .

amnesia
is the only form that knows how to take on color

II

numbered wind
gusting from blue to paler blue
though it's where we begin, it's not what matters

it becomes no different from what follows
which is a newborn instantly threatening to freeze up
an expression extracted here where it's become difficult
to breathe, to write

a broadening spray

. . .

writing is based only on what gives way

writing through weakness, into the yellow, to open the heart
one hand in artifice, the other in the dark
and perfect pitch tuned to grammar

to write or to write

be it drowned or struck
never in the womb of a conjunction
always pain upon pain

. . .

so precise it can find the scene in the dead of night
memory to heel

parts the branches

never resigned to forgetting

. . .

overwhelming anthill

or all the words you don't know
just air in mid-air

I, too, am looking for a naked yellow
the unprotected
the one that contradicts its name

that's only known by its projected shadow
like a spring

a hyper-ripe yellow propagating from yes to yes
a world all pieced together, incurable

the solidified billions
as if neither light nor motion
still asked to be divided

. . .

yellow has no definite edges, its precision is internal
and because green begins right beside it

the borders are constantly shifting
the line between predator and victim

to circumscribe a sensation
would be to list the consequences of coincidence
to wander the corridors of a lightning bolt
to become methodically mute amid words

so many blind months, so many lettered colors

held inside the unsealing
until it holds

yellow become a constraint

not obsessive, simply separate
knotted and knotted
as necessary as the *jouissance* of the woods

. . .

without knowing how the point of view was shattered

sentence passed through a sieve
cutting across the insensible

the eye, the sentence, tarnished by the breath of perspective.

nothing came before
neither in the forest
nor in the shadow of language

yellow first and first the mountain

. . .

the flow is not the same

despite the rules, there's a first sentence

skinned alive

we're all faced with the same condition:
a leap, a defeat
and Scotch broom

which can't be planned, not in writing
nor in memory

being is already a violent detour

and and and
heart and contour
of the chance of letting go

the stand of broom eases the passage
it rips up whatever thinks that sight can reach

direct mourning of the *and*
mourning and emanation

. . .

the eyes will want contraction
a crowd on the pink path

the sentence says it sideways, hoping for backwards
like the body excited by yellow
that yellow extends and enlivens

getting more uncertain and more piercing

in the fleeting intensity:
fleece-yellow, pushing outward, plot

. . .

by going through the woods   I become no longer
the hill's owner
sharper of glance

a body
kinetically fading to yellow

an agrammatical yellow that unwinds

like taking a verb with its color
and finding that the hill becomes objective

often: the terminals are missing
no new news

then shoulders bear us away, gravely

shoulders as a kind of transubstantiation
the shoulders let us fall

there where forest and sentence will co-exist

. . .

The bold figures I write are invented
a labyrinth that will wipe out inherited images

and possibly even language

. . .

a yellow of hands once done without return

meta-yellow event
and its imprint

IV

Resemblance holds sway only as long as it's not explicit.
There's a body missing. It will not be returning.
The stand of broom has awakened a hinge. The yellow, in itself a
consequence, remains to be determined . . .

. . .

Body on the ridge, blending in here and there.
Yellow to grind for two empires and a burn.
To make sure that the resemblance doesn't escape us, I must write
like you. Yellow must carry you away, must initiate us and make us
suffer, and it must remain out of reach, which is to say, stay truly there,
outside.

. . .

The stand of broom is neither always available, nor anarchically named. It is
a stretch of bright yellow that shudders, and a ghost. It's the ghost
that grows and this growing is an abyss of love.
Yellow as if to say   cannot be gathered.
Yellow ankle whose appearance detaches like the murmur from a sentence.

That sort of poem.
Yellow and yellow outside.
A strictly liquid outline.

. . .

I'm trying for a description that could hold out a bouquet, that could offer
you this public yellow and this privation.
I insist that writing lead not only to a moving end
but that it also mark an ascension, a nervous terminus that mumbles
in the field with branching fangs.

. . .

Something inconsolable. A cognitive pain. A poem like that.
That tracks reason down wherever it's insoluble, wherever it can't be
ratified: beyond sensation and beyond broom. Turning back until the yellow
is intact.

Broom filmed breathlessly; the yellow stirred up and stored.
To revive without erasure is to remember.
To live is to turn instantly yellow.
Yellow, impeded by something piercing, that the sentence equals.

. . .

Color, that which burns the story. Like hill invented,
hill ancestral and bristled,
engraved by fingernail and candlelight, without writing.

. . .

Yellow rips out our desire for tomorrow. Yellow swarming in the bowl.
The vanilla-ed sentence exits the shadow, reflecting.
According to a certain logic, it's building castles
of new lines in the Spain of earth, lines of dawn, colors that mount.
Logic is a double-bladed weapon, escorting a body
over a void, pinned down by the throttling yellow, by abduction.

v

Brutally, near Roche Chérie, after dark, June 18, I'm at the movies.

A sequence in the life of eyes that sheds whatever surrounds them; snapshot moving in its perfect black and white, its cloak, its rings.

That crosses, that stops, that vanishes in the headlights.

. . .

Seen, who sees me, who sees my luminous machine, whose eyes gleam within, who rushes into the black with its white stripes.

. . .

Never seen one before, not even aware of its existence, not even its name linked incredibly to my pursuit:

Une genette.

Or a male. No yellow. Only B & W. An old film, restored; clear to counting the pixels of the animal's eyes.

. . .

Ringed poem. Poem that slinks away.

Forest charging down; from the heart of my launch, from my yellow
scratching at the bone.
Crossing the road. Fur gilded, luxurious, geometric tail, without an ounce
of color. . .
The English civet cat stops in my headlights.

The Cat of the Genet.

. . .

Appearing and disappearing in the hallucinatory non-yellow, flashed, fixed in
the elsewhere.

. . .

Above all, no tale, no myth. The test of a wall. the test of serenity ascending
through language. Of pain.
A yellow that already, at the point of departure, no longer exists.

Never even saw it coming. Put that in writing. Augment the visual.
And one fine evening, in ultra-chic B & W, passing the stand of broom in recompense.
Printing memory out striped.

. . .

Hypnotic eyes.
Unstapling weather; grafting beyond-language.

It such as.

Disappeared, cross.

. . .

Sensation goes metallic. Advances through the hardened language.
Making sure the body doesn't get off lightly.

Ordinary language, discoloring. Regulating no accounts,
stitching the treaty. Suddenly, you no longer hear the woods.
You wander amnesia easily in a supple skirt. Yellow immersion.

To the point that the force of the visual begins in its unfurling. In coming
on the hill.

. . .

One foot in color, the other in expression.
One word in the sentence, one in the throat.

That yellow reads itself without being seen.

I burn the bridges so that the uninterrupted heartbreak of the connection
is set adrift.

So that it never gets there.
Passing from one to the other, without having to walk.

Can be projected as soon as a screen. The screen is arranged to end the divinity of collisions.

Though the sentence may seem natural, it's only an inversion.
A projection.
An exceptionally photogenic B & W.

Paralleled by cicadas that sound like falling water.

Crucial and luminous footbridge. Without beyond. Pure romance.

Then it left me.

VI

Writing:
the only good moments are the bursting through
the expulsion

the bright yellow of Maïakovski's coat

...

to leap on the neck of the obstacle
of the strong-shouldered grammar

to bring the power
of the eyes together with
the entrance of color and the joy of night.

this will be either a sentence or a proposition

propositions are much rarer
more alcoholic
day breaks inside, up to the vertebrae
and out comes rigidity

. . .

if something is seen
it's because something else has been deleted
flogged as if it clung to me
a love-suit

my poor leech left for dead

. . .

p : the proposition, the shortest
the vast, which condenses

that its color be disconnected

in planned forestation
sentences frequent anarchy
they have a between-the-lines wisdom

then they touch p and vibrate
luscious, as language delights
over things not quite
where it flounders

. . .

a well-lit name
a laying on of hands and an injection

color that pearls, hands joined

"words without thoughts never go to heaven"

we're thrilled to see lost in the sky:
gods, lines
the power of wild game

. . .

how to repair what language has sundered
extract the warmth and the wound

but not there where things mix
with words alone

dream-yellow
and yellow that I dream of leaving

hoarded skin
that light crashes on

impregnable yellow

the only thing that can grapple with p
drain it of sky
is

        the line

bold and unprecedented
the porcelain singer

  . . .

all that's carried away passes so quickly

and you're left stunned
with the yellow on the other side

the image is an image lost

lightning's forceps
this mode of praise and pain

nothing holds its tongue and then the hill is simply there
dynamited from everywhere
the heavy hip

  . . .

words see something else
too
too they strip

firing up the maddened clouds
derailing a kiss

and could they be aiming at something without a body?

blackthorn, rose hip

everything about the stand of broom is experimental
the unvanquished yellow
angels

. . .

it   the oriole   the rocket
planting thought

. . .

on tiptoe I come back to
what, without a word, without outside
will have been

founded in destruction

lost from sight:
the screw turns opaquely inside the light
and resonance ends

a wedge against which night
returns to build its depth

. . .

the view has turned to words
YELLOW will be this hunger

it's been a long time since the oriole left

the ax cuts in two, then in three
what's split was not contingent
but the same

yet there are two rifts intertwined
the yellow of YELLOW
−or how that which is written becomes in time visible−

and that which asks for whom
why this bodily alarm

the broom falling into oblivion

splintering color is the first revolt
that angers the angering earth
the walker
who leaves you

I raise my arm
and then it leaves me

and so silence doesn't stop the pain
but internal speech is a root
that can't be grasped without that silence

a heart that speech furrows
and light excises

it's been a long time since description ran up against a wall
since the words *in memoriam*
depended on shock

. . .

my only transgression
has been to trample
the rapacious view again and again

the seamstress of energy

yellow on yellow
scraping the depths

I went to yellow to be revived
and yellow starved me

p blocked me
p said that there will never be another
such amber

I slowed the train of description down to death

. . .

I repeat: this color stretches out
and you can always start from there

September 5th: slippery sky

. . .

it's the play of mist and sun

transparent through levels
as in p, dawn and tomb, recurrent breakthrough

of rain, of folded matter
that together infiltrate the phrase

because the search covers every zone of existence

moving strip of color wanted
but mute, clinging to its echo

shot, in the dust
dragging well behind its rapture

. . .

the earth didn't change direction
upon the arrival of the first word
but night filled up with roots

more radiant to face
irremediably frontal, visceral

. . .

a flower cut into flesh
a laborious flower

of the broom
one draws a breath
on what, under the skin

who

the sentence that

a striped line, a striped land

I would have liked it tinted yellow
and shined

the hill's grey
mid-way through the body

composite, causative

whirlwind on the right
nothing moving on the left

. . .

wanting want to rise up in the brain
and oust

the grasshopper's haunches
singing stalk
all my gathered yellows

it's time to hand over slowly
augmenting the animal

losing the balance in stone
a grain of yellow blown up a thousand times
what you get does not look like

listen, we're numerous
all lit

About the Author

Nicolas Pesquès is the author of over ten volumes of poetry and creative nonfiction; his last several books focus on a mountain called Juliau in the Ardèche region of south-central France. The current volume is a section of *La face nord de Juliau, cinq*, as is another book available in English translation under the title of *Physis* (Free Verse Editions, 2006). *La face nord de Juliau, six* was published in 2008. He has also written extensively on visual artists, including Gilles Aillaud, Aurelie Nemours, Anne Deguelle, and Paul Wallach. Active for years in animated films, he has produced versions of *Tintin* and *Asterix*, among others. He currently lives in Paris.

About the Translator

Cole Swensen's recent books include *Ours* (2008), *The Book of a Hundred Hands*, *The Glass Age*, *Noon*, *Try*, *Oh*, and *Such Rich Hour*. She has translated Pierre Alferi, Olivier Cadiot, Pascalle Monnier, Jean Frémon and others. Both her poetry and her translations have won many prizes. She teaches at the Iowa Writers' Workshop.